# quiet moments

## Patricia T. Holland

**DESERET BOOK**

SALT LAKE CITY, UTAH

From a chapter in A *Quiet Heart*, by Patricia T. Holland (Salt Lake City: Bookcraft, 2000).

Visit us at deseretbook.com

ISBN 1-59038-398-2

Printed in United States of America                                         71737
Precision Litho, Salt Lake City, UT

10   9   8   7   6   5   4   3   2   1

*C*hrist is "the light of the sun . . . the moon . . . the stars . . . and the earth also, . . . which light proceedeth forth from the presence of God to fill the immensity of space. . . . The day shall come when you shall comprehend even God, being quickened in him and by him. Then shall ye know that ye have seen me, that I am, and that I am the true light that is in you, and that you are in me; otherwise ye could not abound" (D&C 88:7–10, 12, 49–50).

Every human heart desires to "abound" in God. That can come only through the light by which God quickens us. Illuminated hearts become filled with charity—for ourselves, for others, and for God, who perpetuates that cycle until charity fills the emptiness of any space. Therefore the Lord tells us, "Above all things, clothe yourselves with the bond of charity" (D&C 88:125).

We cannot give love or strength that we do not ourselves have. So if we expect to clothe ourselves with the bond of charity—if we hope to bless others with God's truths and compassion and sustenance—then we must spend more time with God in a very direct way. We do not have to rely on anyone else's witness of the Father. We can have direct encounters of our own. As Paul told the Ephesians, we can literally be "filled with all the fulness of God" (Ephesians 3:19). Those encounters can fill and refill our cups every day of our lives.

Paul's promise seems especially relevant because more and more we live in a world that can be frighteningly empty. Those who don't have the gospel, both near home and around the globe, often create ineffective communities, work in stress-filled professions, and have declining morals, ruined health, failing families, and in the end, failing hope.

One especially troubling complaint of our time is there is no commonality among women. Across cultures and countries and even in our own neighborhoods, we women have become so diverse and so separated in our lifestyles, interests, and preoccupations that rarely do we have a friend such as our mothers had over the back fence, a neighbor to visit, to love, and to talk with. But we still need someone to listen when our joints ache, our children squabble, or (perhaps even more urgently) when we wish we had squabbling children or loved ones nearby to nurture. We must not let the modern world isolate, fragment, or distance us from those we can love and serve.

Isolation can be one of the most frightening and stressful circumstances of the human heart. We all need other people and strong, sweet relationships. The Church helps us with that. Relief Society offers us a sisterhood that we can cherish, an association with others who believe what we believe, who hope what we hope, and who love the things of God.

To receive the fulness God has intended for us, to offset the emptiness of isolation or hurt or sorrow, to clothe ourselves "with the bond of charity, as with a mantle" (D&C 88:125), we are all going to have to reach out with our hearts and let down some barriers. Most of us protect ourselves from pain—hurtful experiences and words that come from our friends, our enemies, and sometimes from within us—by building walls, emotional defenses around our hearts.

But the same walls we build to protect ourselves can also isolate us, and that isolation leads to the problems we see so many others struggling with. Can we let down a few walls and find that we are in the embrace of God? Let's receive the spirit of holiness and let our cups be filled with living water. Let us receive in order to give.

One of my foundation stones for trusting that this can happen is a powerful statement from President George Q.

Cannon: "No matter how serious the trial, how deep the distress, how great the affliction, [God] will never desert us. He never has, and He never will. He cannot do it. It is not His character. He is an unchangeable being; the same yesterday, the same today, and He will be the same throughout the eternal ages to come. We have found that God. We have made Him our friend, obeying His gospel; and He will stand by us. We may pass through the fiery furnace; we may pass through deep waters; but we shall not be consumed nor overwhelmed. We shall emerge from all these trials and difficulties the better and purer for them, if we only trust in our God and keep His commandments" (*Collected Discourses,* comp. Brian H. Stuy [B. H. S. Publishing, 1988], 2:185).

I would place that theology right at the heart of the gospel. We have every right to be hopeful. We have every right to have faith. God lives and loves us. He will not desert us. We can let down a few of our defenses against a faithless world.

Paul wrote, "*Be not conformed to this world:* but be ye transformed by the renewing of your mind, that ye may prove what is that good, and acceptable, and perfect, will of God" (Romans 12:2; emphasis added). To connect with God and be filled with his fulness, to resist conforming to the world, and to discover "that good, and acceptable, and perfect, will of God" *for us* requires a settled, calm mind, a "renewed mind," as Paul suggests, a spirit of contentment, a divine trust and serenity, and a willingness to surrender to God's will. A renewed mind is one that has been illuminated by a new spiritual perception—revelation. When our minds have been illuminated to see as God sees, it becomes a joy to accept his will.

At a time when my eldest son was still single and wanting so much to be married, I was anxiously pleading with the Lord to bless him. My request was very specific; I knew what my son needed. As I was pleading (with an eye fixed on my needs and my anxieties), asking the Lord to please bless him, the words came resoundingly into my mind, "I *am* blessing him. Be patient with my plan." I was stunned—moved to tears. I realized I had been commanding heaven, saying, "Lord, here is your work as I have outlined it. Please notify me when you have bestowed my blessings, pursued my plans, and carried out my will."

In sweet reply comes the mild rebuke, "If you don't mind, Patricia, I prefer to bestow my blessings and to do it in my way." When we can feel sure that God has not forgotten us—nor will he ever—and that he is blessing us in his own way, then the world seems a better, safer place. If we can be patient with his process—which simply means having faith—if we can commune personally and often with him, we can spare ourselves the emptiness and frenzy we feel if we are "conformed to the world": fainthearted, impatient, troubled by envy or greed or pride of a thousand kinds. We can keep our minds fixed enough on eternity to remember that God's ways are not our ways (see Isaiah 55:8–9).

Isn't it sometimes discouraging to see just how easily the adversary uses such earthly issues as vanity and worry, envy and pettiness to distract us from our divine mission and the unity we could enjoy in the Church? We all get discouraged and distracted—caught up in the thick of thin things—no matter how good we are. But do we have time, energy, or emotion to waste on what dress to wear or whose living room is the loveliest? We have real things to think about, things of the kingdom of God. We need to drink more deeply and be filled more fully for the work that lies ahead of us.

Let me suggest some ways that this fulness can come. Often when I face difficulties, I need to turn off the phone, lock the door, kneel in earnest prayer, and then curl up in a chair and meditate, contemplate, search the scriptures, and cry out again and again in my heart, completely focusing my mind on the mind and will and presence of God until I can see a clear picture of him. I like to think of him with loving, outstretched arms. With such a loving image, I begin to feel my connection with him and a confirmation of his love. Sometimes I may have to work at this for hours, for a significant portion of the day, or for several days.

Now, I can just hear you saying, "Pat, get real. I don't have five minutes to do that, let alone an hour or two. I am exhausted now just trying to keep up with things." I know all about your life because it is my life, too. I am busy also, and I have been for as long as I can remember. I know what it is like to chauffeur teenagers, face the laundry, serve in the Church and in the community, and be married to one of the Lord's equally busy servants. But that has *everything* to do with the point I wish to make.

I realize that life has to go on and that you will not be able to pursue this heavenly communication in a completely uninterrupted way, but if it is a high priority and a fundamental goal in your life, you will find ways, early or late, to be with God. If the key to your car or your mortgage payment check or a child were lost, would you take time to find them? Wouldn't finding them provide the peace you needed to then go about your day? If God is lost from your life and you are not going to be strong or stable without him, can you be focused and fixed enough to find him?

If you believed that your earthly father could comfort any heartache, heal any illness, solve any problem, or just be with you through the crucibles of life, wouldn't you call to him constantly? I am just childish enough to believe that our Father in Heaven can bless us in all those ways. The price to be paid for this kind of communion is time and your best powers of concentration, but by that investment you may offset untold hours, days, weeks, and months of struggle or sorrow or pain.

For me, sometimes this communing with God has to be early in the morning—that is my best time—when I am fresh and revelation is strong. Occasionally it has to be at night before I go to bed. In any case, it has to be when things are still, when the house is quiet and my mind is calm. I have the good fortune on those early mornings or late nights to have an unobstructed view of the beautiful Bountiful Temple just three-quarters of a mile from my home. As I look at the temple I see first its holiness, its brightness, beauty, and light. Whether rain or snow is falling, whether the clouds are low and hovering or the sun is bright overhead, the temple is lovely and firm. Its immovable quality steadies my soul—particularly on those days when I seem so very movable and so very drawn and driven in many directions. Its strong, straight spire reminds me that, unlike the temporal things in my life, my health and the demands of the day and the laundry waiting to be done, the real me—the spiritual me, the real Pat Holland, the divine in me—is firm and fixed and stable and settled, like that temple on that hill. I take great comfort in the thought that the things that swirl around us are not us and that the demands on our lives are *not* life itself.

President Gordon B. Hinckley has spoken frequently of meditation. My husband has commented on how often, in speaking to the First Presidency and the Quorum of the Twelve, President Hinckley has asked that they make sure they take time for thoughtfulness, for pondering, for introspection, for meditation. He often refers to a statement of President David O. McKay: "Meditation is the language of the soul. It is defined as 'a form of private devotion, or spiritual exercise, consisting in deep, continued reflection on some religious theme'" (in Conference Report, April 1946, 113).

Somewhere in our lives there must be time and room for such personal communion. Somewhere in our lives there must be time and room for the celestial realities we say we believe in—or when will millennial peace be ours?

The kind of contemplation, reflection, and yearning for God I am speaking of can't be accomplished very handily in competition with cellular phones, computers, or a blaring TV. God can enter our realm only at our invitation. He stands at the door and knocks always, but someone has to hear that knock and let him enter. In this effort we ought to do whatever we can to make our houses—or our apartments or our condominiums—the temples, quite literally, that God intends them to be. Places for the Spirit of the Lord to dwell. Places for meditation, contemplation, prayer, and study. Places where good conversation and charity out of a pure heart can be present. Places where we find the fulness of God.

We need to simplify and spiritualize and celestialize. If most of what we are doing doesn't fit these categories, if at least some portion of our day is not turned to heaven, then we have a wrenching, rending emptiness awaiting us—isolation of the first order—and we will find no cloak of charity with which to protect ourselves or our sisters. We simply have to see what we can eliminate, what we can replace with something higher and holier, more reflective, compassionate, and eternal. Second only to dedicated temples, our homes are to be the sacred edifices of the Lord, places of peace and holiness and sanctity.

I am not being Pollyannish about this. I have already said that I know very well the demands upon a woman's time. It is because I know them so well that I am speaking as I am. I am speaking not only out of the depths of my heart but also out of the depths of my experience. You can say, "It can't be done. There is too much to do. It takes too much energy." Yes, you can say that—but you may miss forever the divine knock at the door. Or as the scripture says even more poignantly, "The harvest is past, the summer is [over], and [our souls are] not saved!" (D&C 56:16).

I believe a woman seeking the cloak of charity, a woman desiring with all her heart to receive the fulness of God, has a chance to break through these telestial, temporal trappings we hang onto. I believe she can find special powers, sacred powers, to bring to latter-day tasks. Through God she can receive the power to serve and sustain and sacrifice.

Most of us are well acquainted with the responsibilities of service. I am sure many of you have baked cookies until your spatulas melted or baby-sat your neighbor's children until your brains sputtered. Occasionally when I am in such situations I fear my fatigue will slip into resentment, and then I wonder if being stretched so thin may not only prevent my developing new charity but actually diminish the supply I thought I had. I have learned, however, that though we may not have a completely willing heart every time we serve, such service molds our heart, blesses us, and enlarges our capacity to give. We must remember, too, during periods of our lives in which we feel that all we can do is keep our own immediate circle of families or friends afloat, that *emotional and spiritual* service to others can sometimes be as important as physical acts.

My daughter, Mary, tells of being assigned to visit teach a friend but procrastinating the visit because her friend, who had three preschoolers and was pregnant with a fourth child, always seemed frazzled and frustrated. Mary knew she would want to shoulder some of her friend's tasks, but she also felt stretched to the limit with two preschoolers of her own, a husband in graduate school, and a demanding Church calling.

The idea of having three more children in her two-room apartment adding to her own children's chaos, even for only a few hours, seemed overwhelming. Yet, partially out of duty, but mostly out of love and a desire to lift her friend's spirits, she regularly offered to tend, clean house, and relieve her of some of her other burdens. Occasionally those offers were accepted; more often they were declined. Even when her friend accepted help, Mary could see little difference in her friend's mood.

One day, when Mary herself was having a particularly exasperating day, she called her friend—in the spirit of good visiting teaching—just to tell her that she couldn't help thinking of her and empathizing with her struggles. During that conversation, Mary sensed a gradual change in that sister's attitude, a kind of happiness she hadn't sensed in her very often.

Near the end of the conversation, her friend admitted to feeling nearly ecstatic to realize that Mary, who seemed to be able to handle everything with grace and goodwill, was having a miserable day. The sister explained, "Mary, I am so grateful. I've never had anyone share their frustrations with me. They are always terribly concerned about mine, and they just know I can't handle any others. Your honesty has made me feel so much better. I didn't think you ever felt frazzled like I do. I have always thought you were perfect. But today I see that you are not so different from me. Maybe I am doing just fine. I don't really need help as much as I just need to know that I am normal. Thanks!" Offering someone our companionship and our honest shared sorrows as well as joys is as important as quickly finishing a physical task for them.

What I wish to affirm is that we do need to charitably share and serve—emotionally and spiritually as well as temporally—but we must fill ourselves at the fountain of living water, at the feet of our Heavenly Father himself, or we have nothing of real strength to give. When we connect with God, then we will connect with others honestly and compassionately. When we pay the price to see God, we become aware of how closely connected we are to each other.

In the book of Revelation, John writes metaphorically of a woman representing the power and righteousness of the kingdom of God. When her life was endangered, she "fled into the wilderness" (Revelation 12:6). God had prepared a place for her, a place of safety and strength and protection. In dark and dangerous days, God will provide for us safe places, even wilderness places (I take that to mean sacred places undefiled by worldly civilization) where he protects us against evil and nourishes us with strength. Please allow yourself to take the time to go to that wilderness retreat now, that sanctuary, if you will—

the temple, your own home, a place of privacy and revelation, a place filled with prayer and meditation and scriptural truths. Allow yourself to turn a few things down and turn a few things off. Seek to position yourself prayerfully in some solitude and serenity to receive the mind of God. Stop what you are so frantically doing and go into your private wilderness. Shut the door, turn out all earthly lights, set aside all earthly sights. Position yourself calmly and quietly in humble serenity until your prayer flows naturally and lovingly. When you feel God's presence, when you feel he is with you, you will be filled with a wonderful strength that will allow you to do anything in righteousness.

Thus filled and strengthened, we can return to the battle, to some inevitable noise and commotion and, yes, even some drudgery. But we do it more happily, more hopefully, more optimistically because we have communed with God and been filled in those quiet moments with his joy, his charity, and his compassion, and we bear something of his light as we return. And because we are filled and strong, we can be a source of light, life, and love for others.